LOUISA F. PESEL'S

HISTORICAL DESIGNS FOR EMBROIDERY

Linen and Cross-stitch

With an Introduction by

ETTA CAMPBELL

London: B. T. BATSFORD LTD

First published, in one volume, 1956
First published in paperback, 1988

ISBN 0 7134 5999 9

Printed and bound in Great Britain by
Anchor Brendon Ltd, Tiptree, Essex
for the publishers B. T. Batsford Ltd
4 Fitzhardinge Street London W1H 0AH

CONTENTS

FOREWORD

I very much appreciate the invitation to write an Introduction to this re-issue of the late Miss L. F. Pesel's embroidery books. I am proud to have the opportunity of paying a tribute to her for her endless patience in making these copies from the old Samplers and so enabling us to know and study the early English designs; and also for all she did to teach, train and encourage some of us to carry on the work she did so much to revive.

I do not consider this counted work lends itself very well to modern designs and I feel it is much more satisfactory to take these lovely old traditional designs and to copy and adapt them to our ideas of today. There is no need for slavish copying. Many good needlewomen find it difficult to design and so are given little encouragement in embroidery. Surely it is better to copy a good design rather than to produce a poor design for good work. How many talented musicians not only give but also gain untold pleasure by interpreting the beauty of song and music, yet only few possess the creative power to compose these works. Why, then, must it be considered essential for every worker to design her own embroidery? Let each do her own part in the whole.

I should advise every prospective embroideress to begin with linen embroidery. It is not difficult to master and it teaches technique (the first necessity for good work) at once by virtue of the counted threads. Why not start off with a sampler, using the various types and stitches in this book? Planning and working a sampler can be most entertaining and the result will produce a very useful "notebook" for further efforts. The name of the worker should always be added, with her home and the date, for posterity.

I believe that if this book were used in our schools, so that British children were taught to use the needle, as the children in this country in earlier ages used it, there would be a revival amongst the younger generation of a love of craftwork. Cross-stitch, especially, appeals to children. It is simple to do and affords a great opening for using colours, so popular with the younger needle-women. I am certain that a child would enjoy planning and working from these charts.

This work has the added value with regard to health, that it needs sufficient concentration to keep the mind occupied without strain and in these days of rush and hurry I believe half an hour each day (within the scope of the busiest) spent in embroidery of this type, would act as a real tonic and rest. In a fairly long experience of teaching I have proved this to be true. If worked reasonably there is no need to fear eyestrain.

I know that this complete volume of designs for the various types of linen embroidery will be a great help to the ever increasing number of workers who are interested in this most absorbing needlework. I believe it will give decided impetus to a very real type of English embroidery, surely more suitable to our temperament than the foreign models so often copied. Furthermore, I am convinced that many needlewomen will derive much pleasure and happiness by working from these charts, and by realising that they are helping to establish once more in this country, the designs and stitches made and worked by their ancestresses long years ago.

Twyford, Winchester,
Winter, 1955

ETTA CAMPBELL

DOUBLE-RUNNING
OR
BACK STITCH

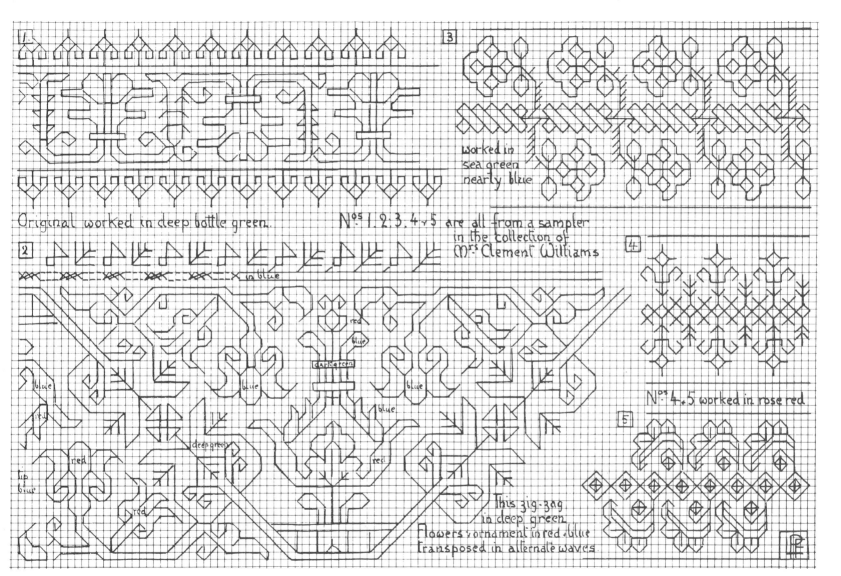

Original worked in deep bottle green.

worked in
sea green
nearly blue

Nos 1. 2. 3. 4. 5 are all from a sampler
in the collection of
Mrs Clement Williams

in blue

red
blue

dark green

blue

blue

blue

blue

Nos 4. 5 worked in rose red

red

deep green

red

red

lip
blue

red

This zig-zag
in deep green

Flowers & ornament in red & blue
transposed in alternate waves.

9

6

7

½ lemon yellow

Zig-zag . leaves green. Flowers 2 red 2 blue 2 red
Strawberries red . yellow . next yellow . red transposed

8

Nos. 6·7·8·9
(Mrs) C. Williams

This is also on V.A.M 516·1877
with the background worked .

10

Stem green . Pale blue flower . dark green leaf . red flower and
yellow green leaf . blue flower . dark green leaf . red flower . pale blue .

9

From 17th century
sampler in the
possession of
the author.
worked in
green.

in nigger
brown.

LP

From an
English sampler
worked by
Isabel Hall
dated
1653
belonging to
Mrs Clement
Williams.

From a
black-work
sampler
formerly in
the possession
of the late
Canon
Greenwell.

II

13

14

in pale blue

in deep blue.

Nos. 13 & 14 are from a 17th century sampler belonging to the author.

15

From an all black-work sampler formerly in the possession of the late Canon Greenwell.

Nos. 16. 17 & 18 (Mrs C. Williams

16

in red

17

in deep blue

18

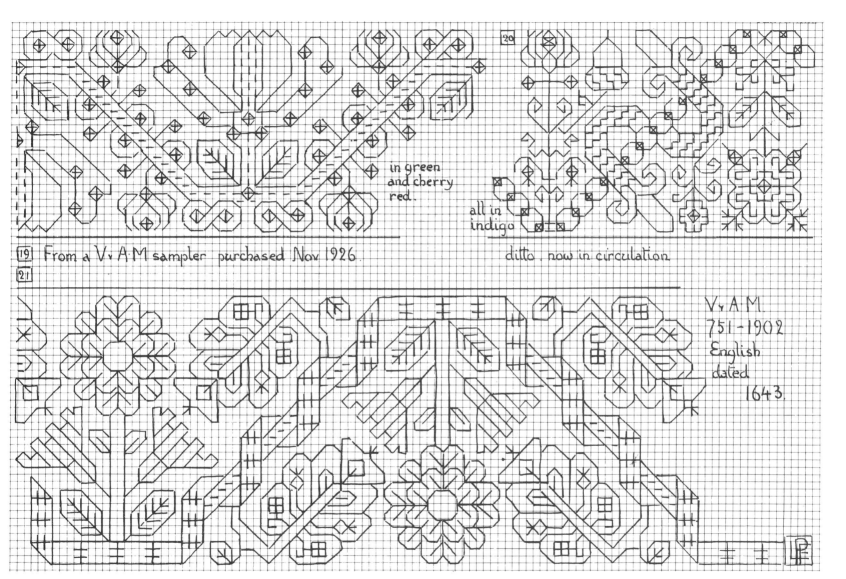

in green and cherry red.

all in indigo

19 From a V.A.M sampler purchased Nov 1926.

ditto. now in circulation

V.A.M
751-1902
English
dated
1643.

22

V.A.M. 751 - 1902

23

24

V.A.M
purchased
Nov: 1926

Flowers red, eyelets green, stem red & green alternate stitches

23

V.A.M
purchased
1926 . now
in circulation
Worked in
deep blue

border green.

V.A.M
751 - 1902
English
dated 1643.

26

scroll ♥ spirals in green.
eyelet flowers red or blue in alternate groups.

From one of Mrs Williams samplers.

28

Worked in green

29

Flowers in blue ♥ red all else green.

27

Nos 26 ♥ 27 are from a 17th century sampler in the possession of the Author.

Nos 26. 29 ♥ 30. from an old sampler copied many years ago by Miss Ravenhill. Worked in red blue ♥ green.

30

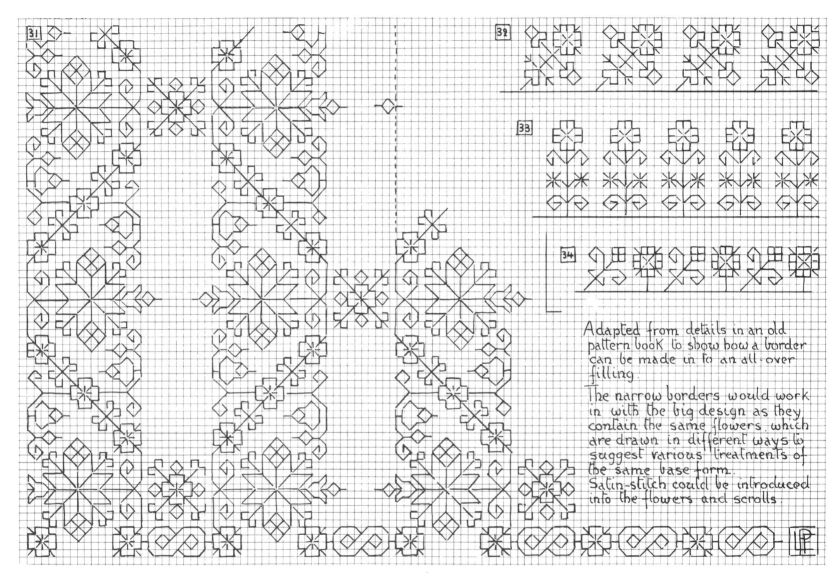

Adapted from details in an old
pattern book to show how a border
can be made in to an all-over
filling.

The narrow borders would work
in with the big design as they
contain the same flowers which
are drawn in different ways to
suggest various treatments of
the same base form.
Satin-stitch could be introduced
into the flowers and scrolls.

Adapted as a filling from
a border on a sampler
belonging to Mrs C. Williams.
The shaded portion shows
two alternative treatments for
the frame-work, which could be
done either in satin stitch or
in some pulled-open, instead
of in the double
running like the
rest of the work.

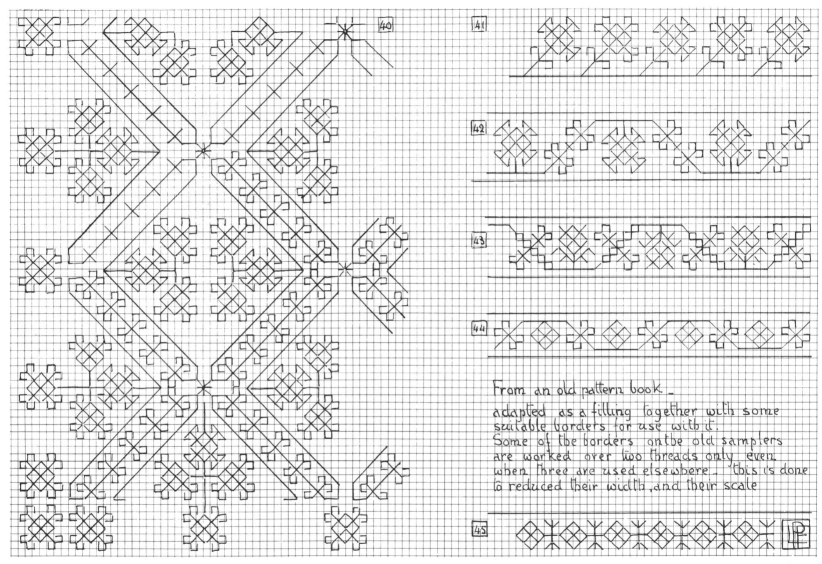

40

41

42

43

44

From an old pattern book –

adapted as a filling together with some
suitable borders for use with it.
Some of the borders on the old samplers
are worked over two threads only even
when three are used elsewhere. This is done
to reduced their width, and their scale

45

18

CROSS-STITCH

1.

2.

3.

Nos 1 to 5 from a sampler V.v A.M. 829 – 1902.

4.

5.

6.

From an old sampler now in the possession of Mrs Longman.

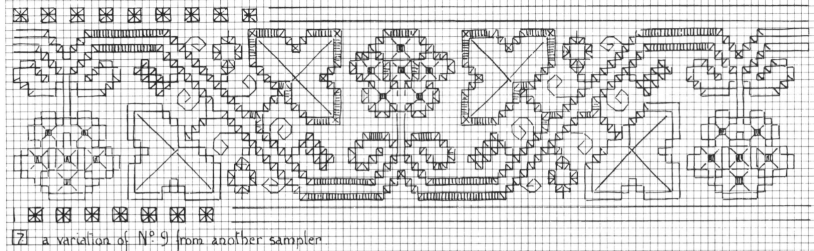

7. a variation of Nº 9 from another sampler

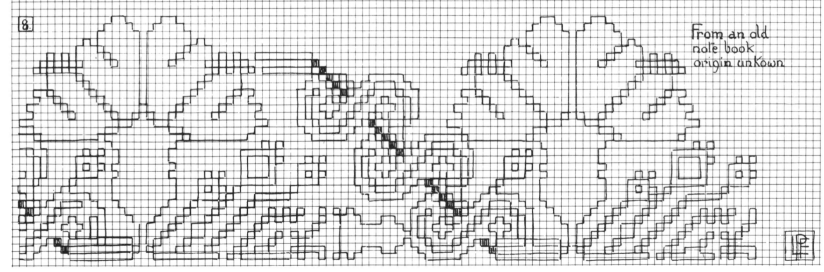

8.

From an old
note book
origin unkown

22

V. & A. M.
741/1899

English
2nd half of
17th century.

V. & A. M.
741-1899

also on a
sampler
formerly
in the
possession
of the late
Canon
Greenwell.

11. V.v.A.M
8-1874

12. V.v.A.M
8-1874
English
dated
1666.

14 V. A. M. 266/1911.

solid   solid

solid

13 V. A. M. 516 - 1877.

15

16

V. A. M. 804 - 1877

darned over 2 threads

Nº 15 From a sampler in the possession of
Mrs Clement Williams

The curved band could be made 2 squares
narrower & the flowers 2 squares wider
if big spaces were required for
pulled fillings.

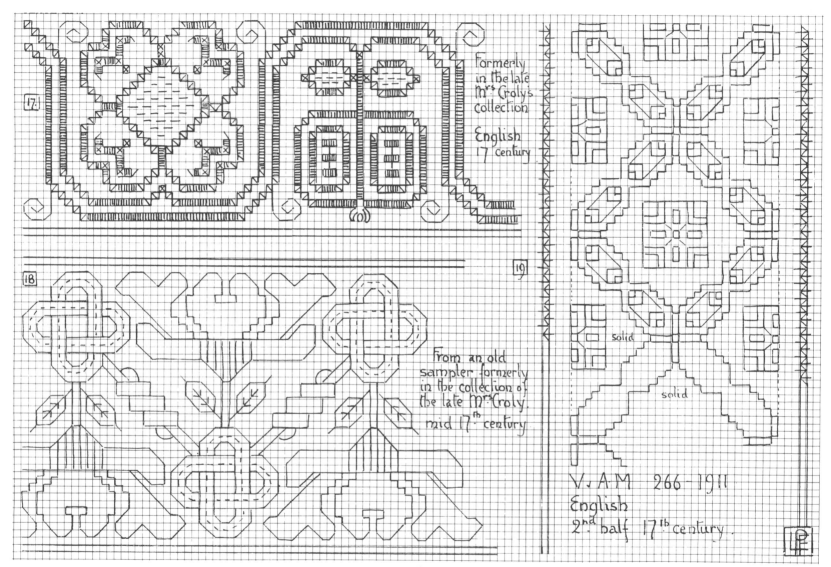

17

Formerly
in the late
Mrs Croly's
collection

English
17 century

(a)

18

19

From an old
sampler formerly
in the collection of
the late Mrs Croly.
mid 17th century

solid

solid

V. A M   266 - 1911
English
2nd half 17th century.

26

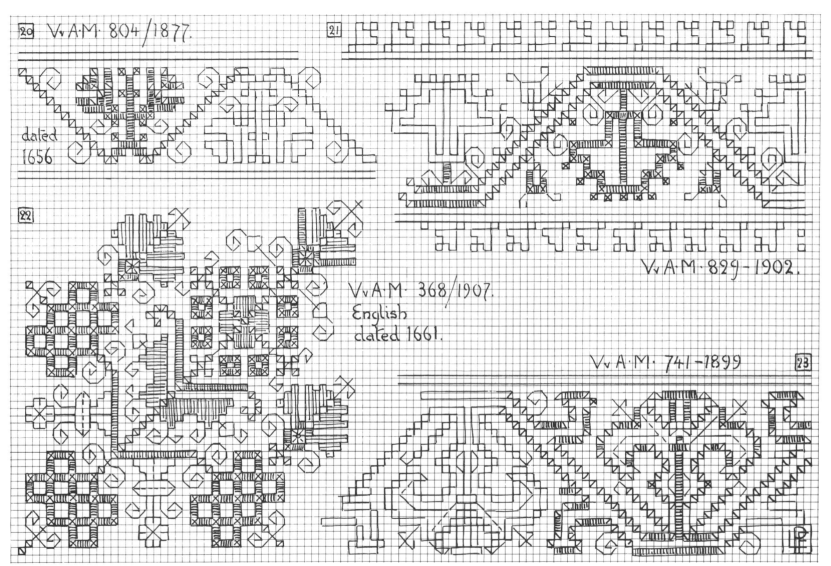

20 V.A.M. 804/1877.

dated 1656

21

22

V.A.M. 368/1907.
English
dated 1661.

V.A.M. 829-1902.

V.A.M. 741-1899

23

24

V.v.A.M. 829 - 1902

25

V.v.A.M 368-1907. dated 1661

V.v.A.M 804 - 1877

26

English
V.v.A.M.
829 - 1902

27

28 V.v.A.M 17ᵗʰ century English.

V.A.M. 829-1902
English
2nd half of 17th century
also with slight variations on
V.A.M. 804-1877
                dated 1656
V.A.M. 480-1894
and on one of Mrs Loongman's
also on samplers illustrated by
Marcus B. Huish in "Samplers &
Tapestry Embroideries"
Plate III & figures 8.18.43.

Alternative square for
use if all solid work
is desired.

30 31

Nos 30 . 32 from a
sampler in the
possession of
Mrs Longman

English
second half of
17th century

V·A·M· 829 – 1902

32

CANVAS EMBROIDERY

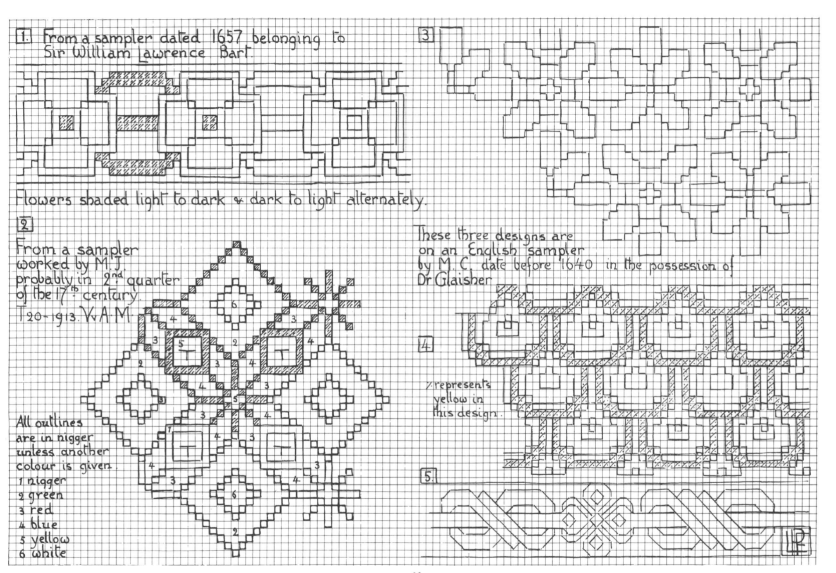

1. From a sampler dated 1657 belonging to
Sir William Lawrence Bart.

Flowers shaded light to dark & dark to light alternately.

2

From a sampler
worked by M.J.
probably in 2nd quarter
of the 17th century.
T20-1913. V.A.M

All outlines
are in nigger
unless another
colour is given.
1 nigger
2 green
3 red
4 blue
5 yellow
6 white

3

These three designs are
on an English sampler
by M.C. date before 1640 in the possession of
Dr Glaisher.

4

⁄ represents
yellow in
this design.

5

33

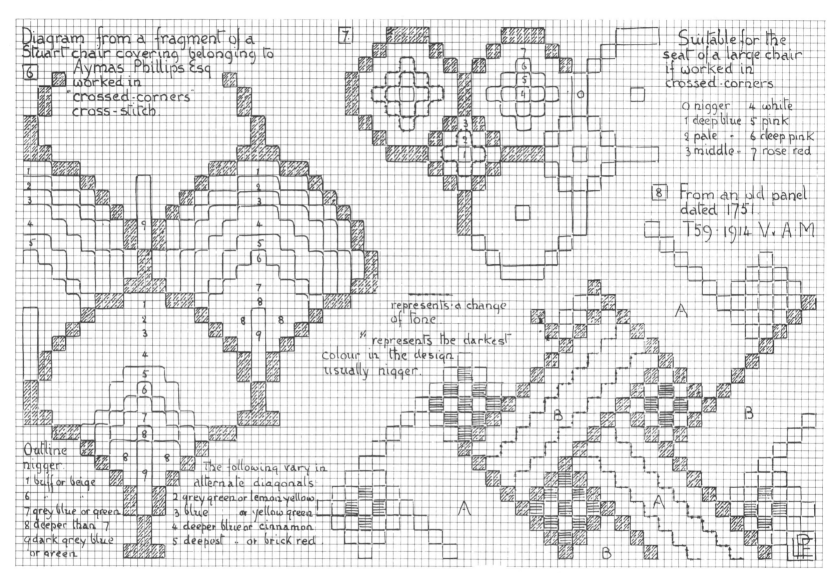

Diagram from a fragment of a
Stuart chair covering belonging to
Aymas Phillips Esq
worked in
"crossed-corners"
cross-stitch.

6

7

Suitable for the
seat of a large chair
if worked in
crossed-corners

0 nigger   4 white
1 deep blue 5 pink
2 pale "   6 deep pink
3 middle "   7 rose red

8 From an old panel
dated 1751.
T59·1914 V·A M

represents a change
of tone.

" represents the darkest
colour in the design
usually nigger.

Outline
nigger.
1 buff or beige
6   "   "
7 grey blue or green
8 deeper than 7
9 dark grey blue
  or green

The following vary in
alternate diagonals
2 grey green or lemon yellow
3 blue   or yellow green
4 deeper blue or cinnamon
5 deepest " or brick red

A

B

B

A

A

B

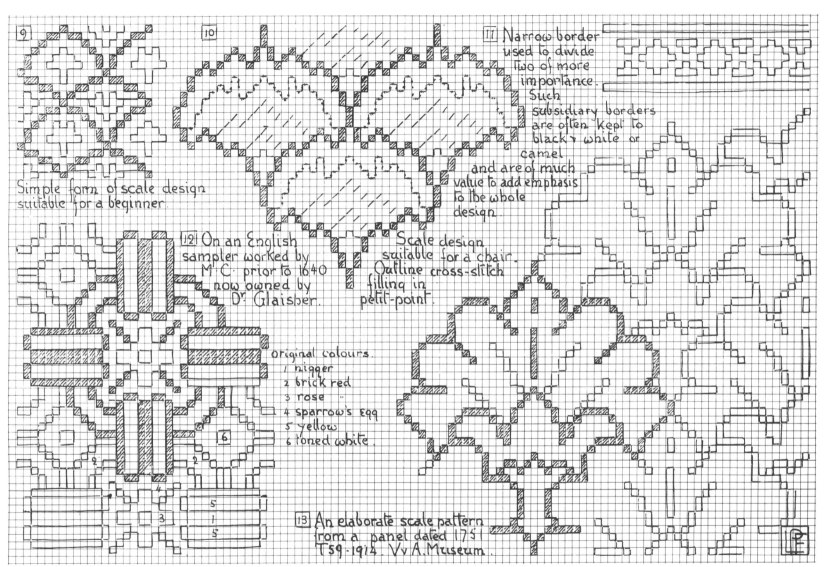

9

10

11 Narrow border used to divide two or more importance. Such subsidiary borders are often kept to black & white or camel and are of much value to add emphasis to the whole design.

Simple form of scale design suitable for a beginner.

12 On an English sampler worked by Mᵣ C. prior to 1640 now owned by Dᵣ Glaisher.

Scale design suitable for a chair. Outline cross-stitch filling in petit-point.

original colours.
1 nigger
2 brick red
3 rose   "
4 sparrow's egg
5 yellow
6 toned white.

13 An elaborate scale pattern from a panel dated 1751 T.59.1914. V & A. Museum.

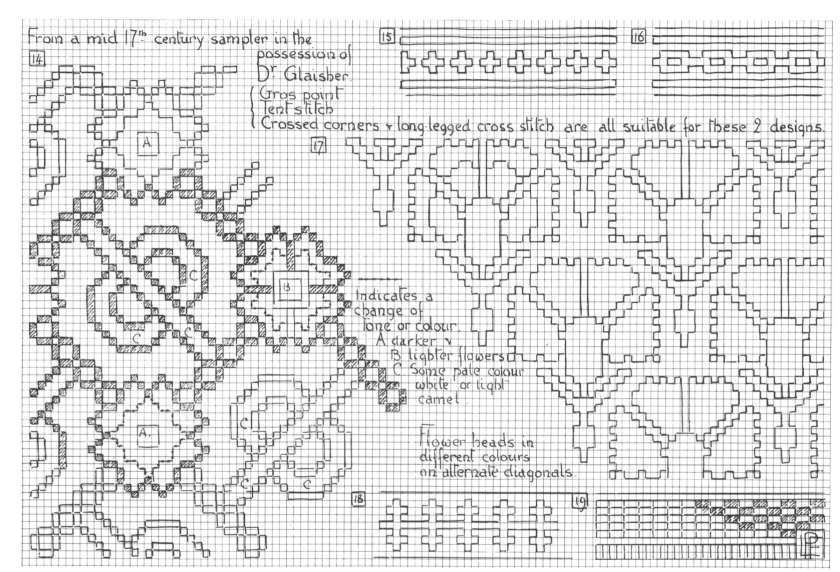

From a mid 17ᵗʰ century sampler in the possession of Dr Glaisber.

{ Gros point
{ Tent stitch
{ Crossed corners & long-legged cross stitch are all suitable for these 2 designs.

14

15

16

17

Indicates a change of tone or colour.
A darker &
B lighter flowers
C Some pale colour white or light camel.

Flower heads in different colours on alternate diagonals.

18

19

A

B

C

36

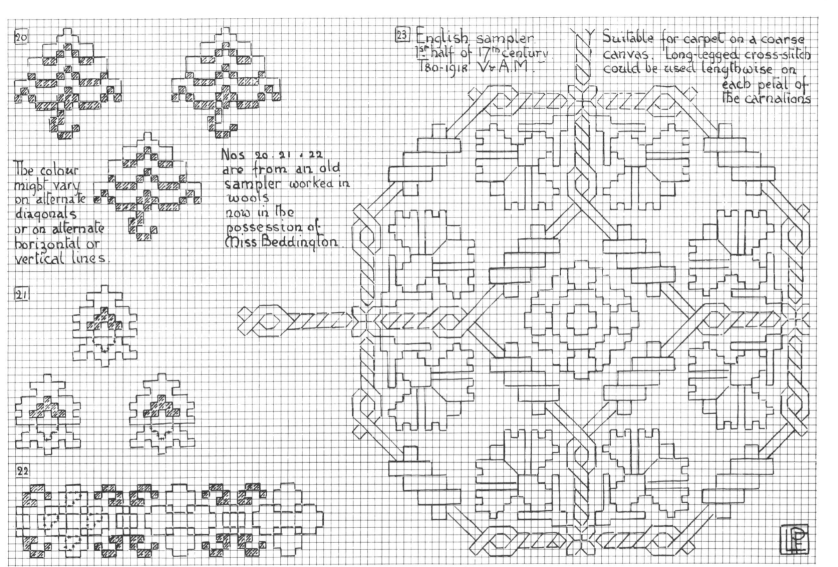

20

23 English sampler
1st half of 17th century
T80-1918 V & A M

Y Suitable for carpet on a coarse
canvas. Long-legged cross-stitch
could be used lengthwise on
each petal of
the carnations

The colour
might vary
on alternate
diagonals
or on alternate
horizontal or
vertical lines.

Nos 20. 21 . 22
are from an old
sampler worked in
wools
now in the
possession of
Miss Beddington

21

22

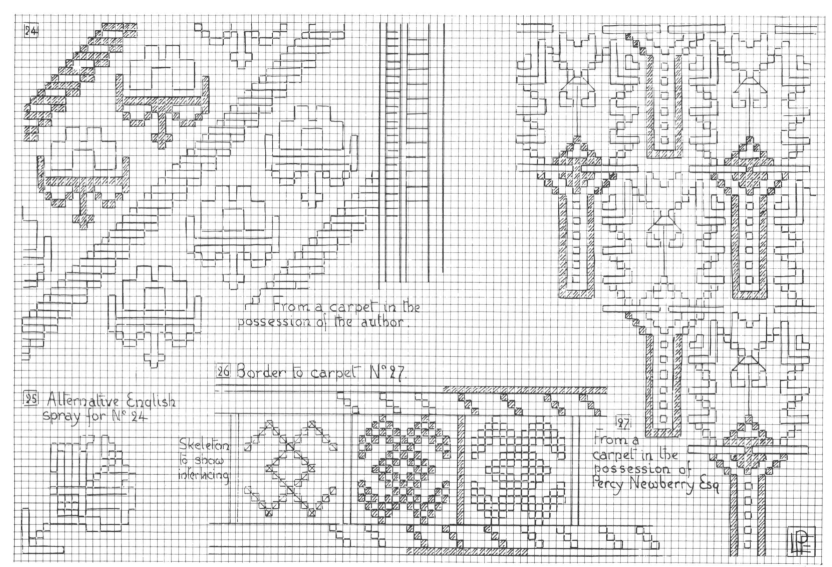

24

From a carpet in the
possession of the author.

26 Border to carpet Nº 27.

25 Alternative English
spray for Nº 24

Skeleton
to show
interlacing

27

From a
carpet in the
possession of
Percy Newberry Esq

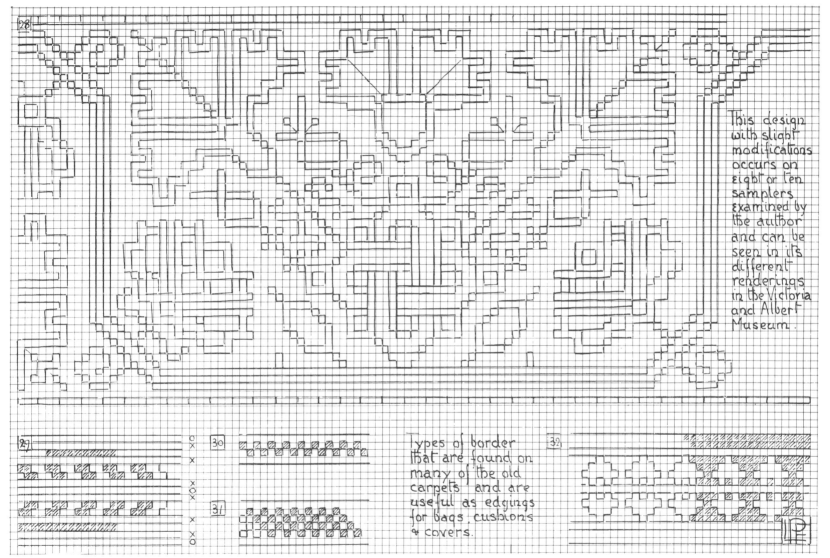

28

This design with slight modifications occurs on eight or ten samplers examined by the author and can be seen in its different renderings in the Victoria and Albert Museum.

29

30

31

32

Types of border that are found on many of the old carpets and are useful as edgings for bags, cushions & covers.

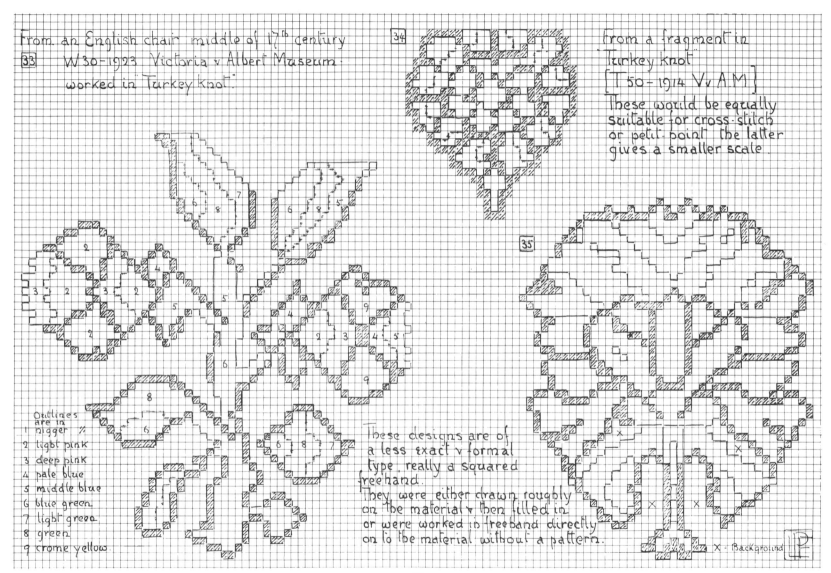

From an English chair middle of 17th century
33 W 30-1923 Victoria v Albert Museum.
worked in Turkey Knot.

34

From a fragment in
Turkey Knot
[T 50 - 1914 Vv A.M]
These would be equally
suitable for cross-stitch
or petit-point the latter
gives a smaller scale.

35

Outlines
are in
1 nigger ?
2 light pink
3 deep pink
4 pale blue
5 middle blue
6 blue green
7 light green
8 green
9 crome yellow

These designs are of
a less exact v formal
type, really a squared
freehand.
They were either drawn roughly
on the material v then filled in
or were worked in freehand directly
on to the material without a pattern.

X - Background

40

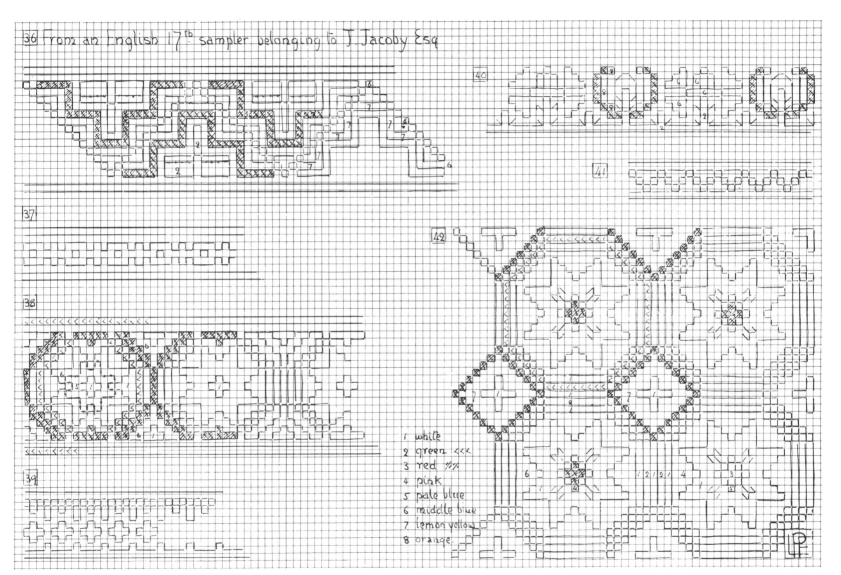

36 From an English 17th sampler belonging to J. Jacoby Esq

37

38

39

40

41

42

1 white
2 green <<<
3 red ///
4 pink
5 pale blue
6 middle blue
7 lemon yellow
8 orange

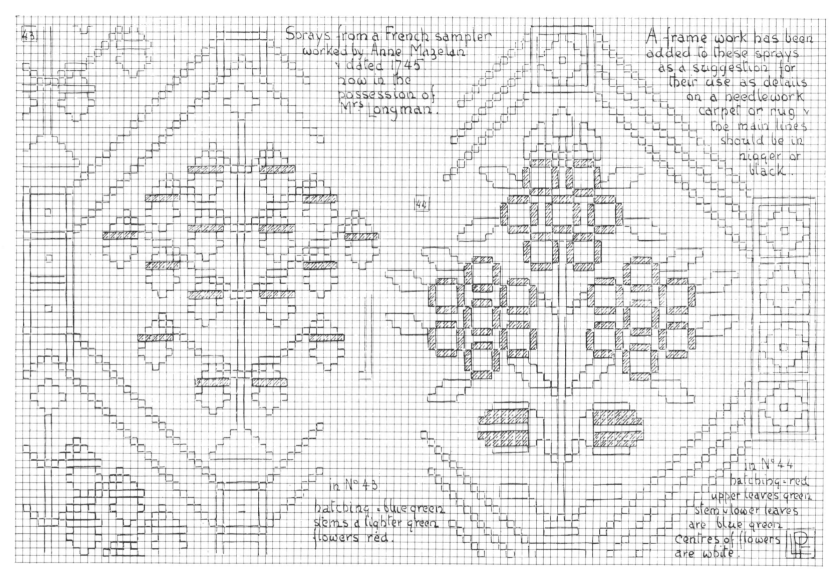

43

Sprays from a French sampler
worked by Anne Mazelan
dated 1745
now in the
possession of
Mrs Longman.

A frame work has been
added to these sprays
as a suggestion for
their use as details
on a needlework
carpet or rug v
the main lines
should be in
nigger or
black.

44

in Nº 43
hatching = blue green
stems a lighter green
flowers red.

in Nº 44
hatching = red
upper leaves green
stem v lower leaves
are blue green
centres of flowers
are white.

LEAVES FROM AN
EMBROIDERY NOTE-BOOK

1. This border over one thread to the square less than the centre same border at the lower edge.

V.A.M. 8-1874 dated 1666.

V.A.M. 266-1911

2. line in over-lapping herring-bone stitch

Several designs on this page were copied from a sampler belonging to the late Canon Greenwell.

4.

berries red. leaves nigger

suitable as a diagonal powdering

suitable for all red, blue or green

3. original in all black, shading some solid surface filling.

V.A.M 516-1877

L.F.P

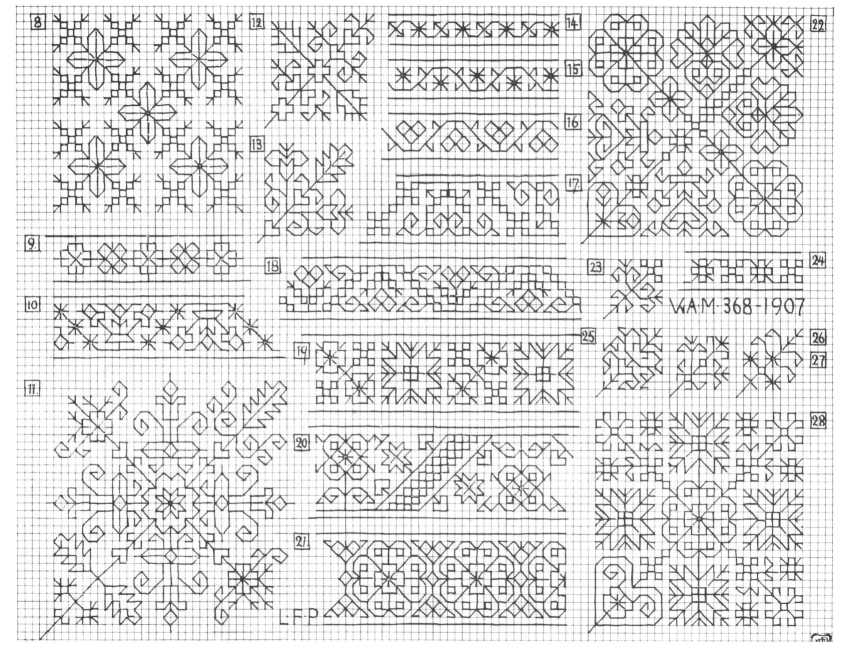

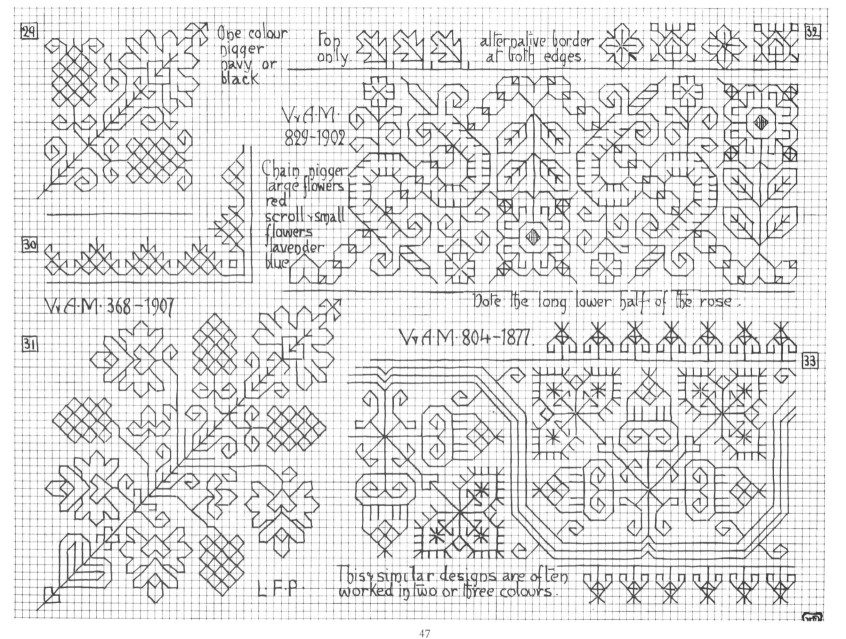

One colour
nigger
navy or
black

Top
only

alternative border
at both edges.

V.A.M.
829-1902

Chain nigger
large flowers
red
scroll small
flowers
lavender
blue

V.A.M. 368-1907

Note the long lower half of the rose.

V.A.M. 804-1877.

This similar designs are often
worked in two or three colours.

L.F.P.

34   Base of acorn in solid filling; upper part & flowers open darning white or pale color

V.A.M 829–1902

English sampler second half of XVII

36   These narrow borders are often over one thread less to the square.

37   38   39

35 V.A.M 516-1877.   V.A.M 829–1902.

Border over one thread less to the square; seven details to one large repeat. Ditto below.

This alternative form has no ribbon, all details are upright.

40

reverse pattern

48

From "A Schole House for the Needle"
pub: in 1632 by Richard SHorleyKer in
England. Squared for double running
from a copy in V&A·M
library

Dote
diagonals
cross over
1 2 3 squares

L·F·P

49

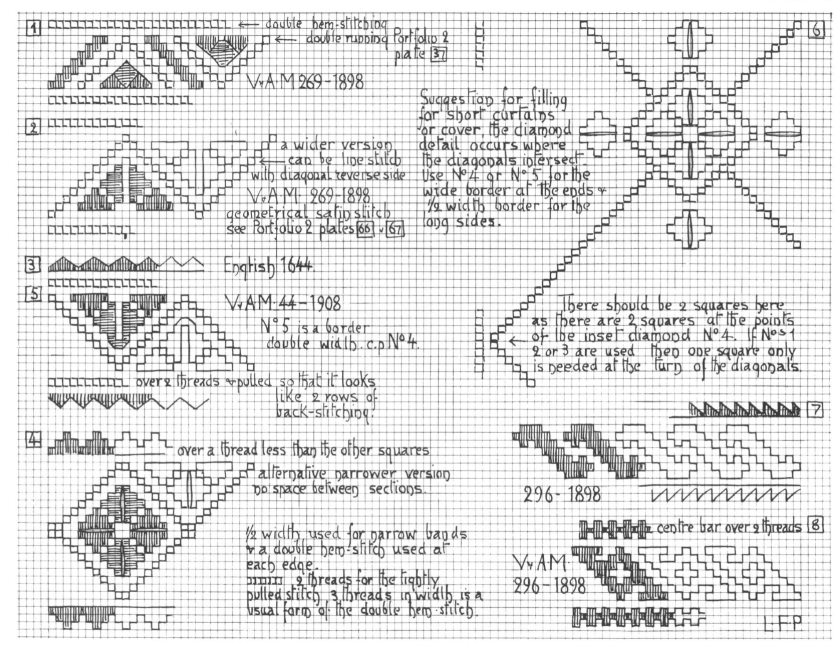

1 ← double hem-stitching
← double running Portfolio 2 plate 37

V.A.M 269-1898

2

a wider version
← can be line stitch
with diagonal reverse side
V.A.M 269-1898
geometrical satin stitch
see Portfolio 2 plates 66 v 67

3 English 1644.

5 V.A.M. 44-1908

N° 5 is a border
double width. c.p N° 4.

over 2 threads v pulled so that it looks
like 2 rows of
back-stitching.

4 over a thread less than the other squares

alternative narrower version
no space between sections.

½ width used for narrow bands
v a double hem-stitch used at
each edge.
2 threads for the tightly
pulled stitch 3 threads in width is a
visual form of the double hem stitch.

Suggestion for filling
for short curtains
or cover, the diamond
detail occurs where
the diagonals intersect.
Use N° 4 or N° 5 for the
wide border at the ends v
½ width border for the
long sides.

6

There should be 2 squares here
as there are 2 squares at the points
← of the inset diamond N° 4. If N°s 1
2 or 3 are used then one square only
is needed at the turn of the diagonals.

7

296-1898

centre bar over 2 threads 8

V.A.M
296-1898

L.F.P

50

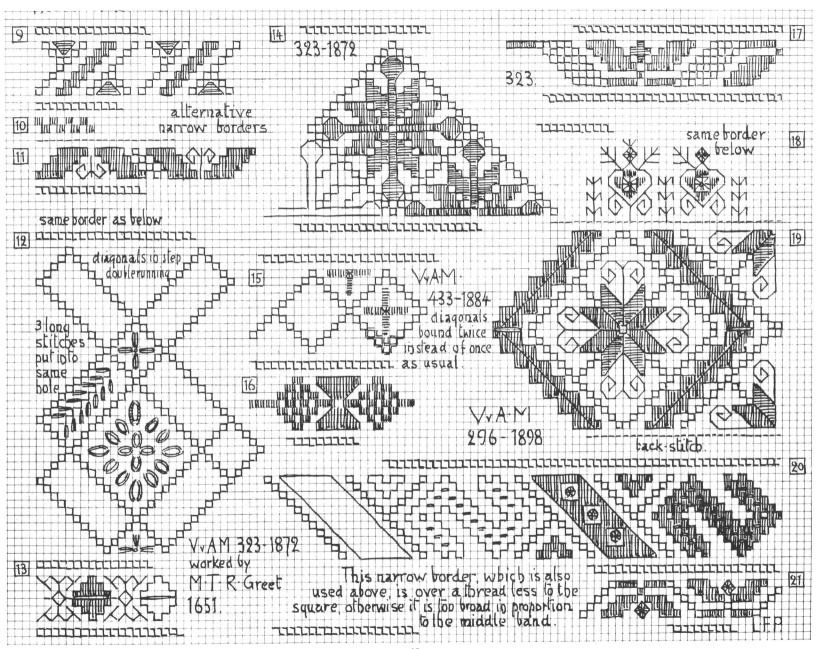

9

14 323-1872

17

323

alternative
narrow borders

10

same border
below

18

11

same border as below

12

diagonals to step
doublerunning

15 V.A.M.
433-1884
diagonals
bound twice
instead of once
as usual.

19

3 long
stitches
put into
same
hole

16

V.A.M.
296-1898

back-stitch.

20

V.A.M 323-1872
worked by
M·T·R·Greet
1651.

This narrow border, which is also
used above, is over a thread less to the
square, otherwise it is too broad in proportion
to the middle band.

13

21

L.F.P.

51

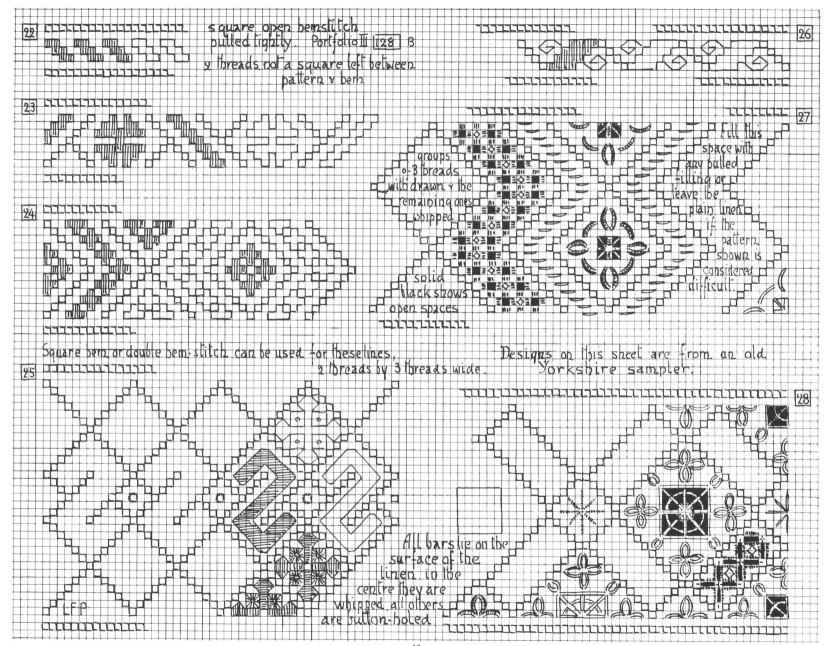

22
square open hemstitch
pulled tightly.   Portfolio III 128 3
9 threads not a square left between
pattern v hem
26

23
27

groups
o-3 threads
with drawn v the
remaining ones
whipped

Fill this
space with
any pulled
filling or
leave the
plain linen
if the
pattern
shown is
considered
difficult.

24

solid
black shows
open spaces

Square hem or double hem stitch can be used for these lines,
2 threads by 3 threads wide.

Designs on this sheet are from an old
Yorkshire sampler.

25

28

All bars lie on the
surface of the
linen. in the
centre they are
whipped all others
are button-holed

L.F.P.

The spacing of these details is unusual giving a broken line.

From an old English sampler in the possession of Sir William Lawrence. Bart

Border Nº 40 matches this design.

satin stitch small eyelet holes

diagonals in double threads i.e. a 2nd whipping before making the next stitch.

53

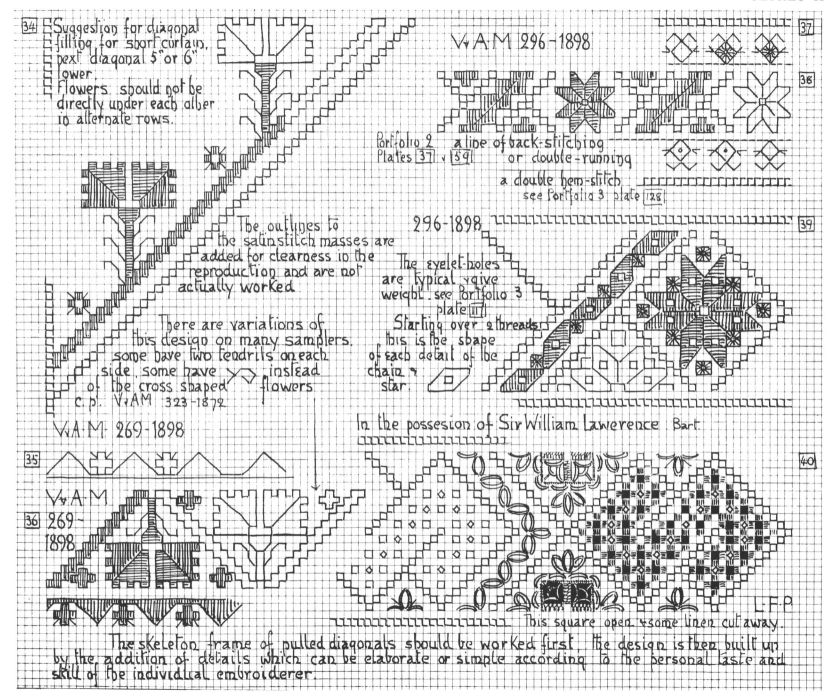

34 Suggestion for diagonal filling for short curtain, next diagonal 5" or 6" lower.
Flowers should not be directly under each other in alternate rows.

V.A.M 296-1898

Portfolio 2   a line of back-stitching
Plates 37 & 59   or double-running

a double hem-stitch
see Portfolio 3 plate 128

The outlines to the satin stitch masses are added for clearness in the reproduction and are not actually worked

296-1898

The eyelet-holes are typical & give weight, see Portfolio 3 plate 11

There are variations of this design on many samplers. some have two tendrils on each side. some have ⋈ instead of the cross shaped flowers
c.p. V.AM 323-1872

Starting over 2 threads this is the shape of each detail of the chain & star.

V.A.M 269-1898

In the possesion of Sir William Lawerence Bart

35

V.A.M
36 269-
1898

40

L.F.P

This square open & some linen cut away.

The skeleton frame of pulled diagonals should be worked first, the design is then built up by the addition of details which can be elaborate or simple according to the personal taste and skill of the individual embroiderer.

V.A.M 476-1897
Spanish sampler
dated 1762.

Three narrow borders
which can be worked
one thread less to the square

Designs on this sheet are from a Spanish sampler
V.A.M 129-1909   dated 1756.

On a fine
linen these
designs are
on the right
scale -

L.F.P.

55

All designs on this page are
from a Spanish sampler
dated 1756
V. A.M 129 - 1909
The originals are in silks
of many colours
but Spanish covers
are also often worked
in a hard brown linen thread, sometimes
in brown & blue.

Stitches
Fishbone Portfolio 1
Plate 12
Geometrical satin stitch
Portfolio 2
Plates 66 67
used below large corner

Spirals in
Stem stitch
Portfolio 1
Plate 1
or double
run
Plate
37

L.F.P.

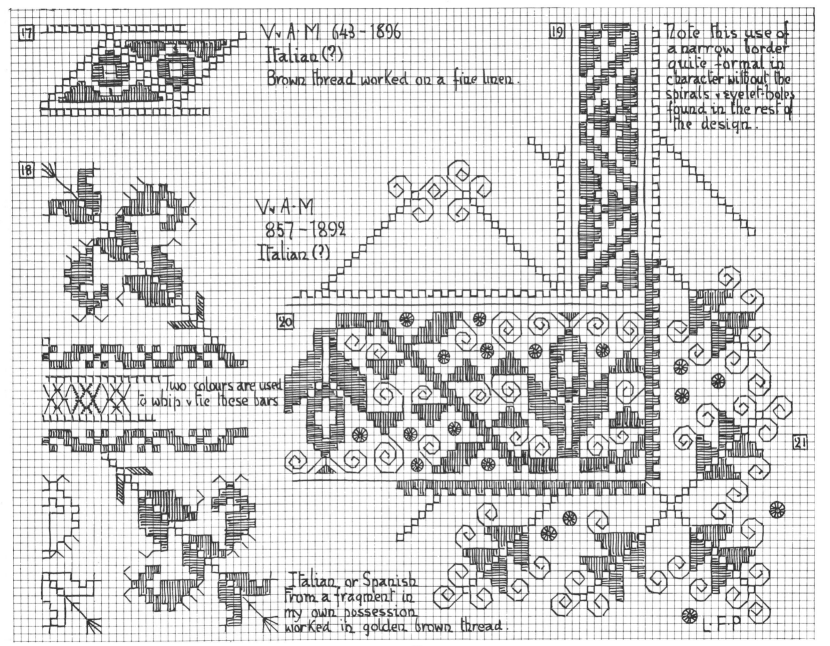

17

V. A. M. 643 - 1896
Italian (?)
Brown thread worked on a fine linen.

18

V. A. M.
857 - 1892
Italian (?)

19

Note this use of
a narrow border
quite formal in
character without the
spirals & eyelet-holes
found in the rest of
the design.

20

Two colours are used
to whip & tie these bars

21

Italian, or Spanish
from a fragment in
my own possession
worked in golden brown thread.

L. F. P.

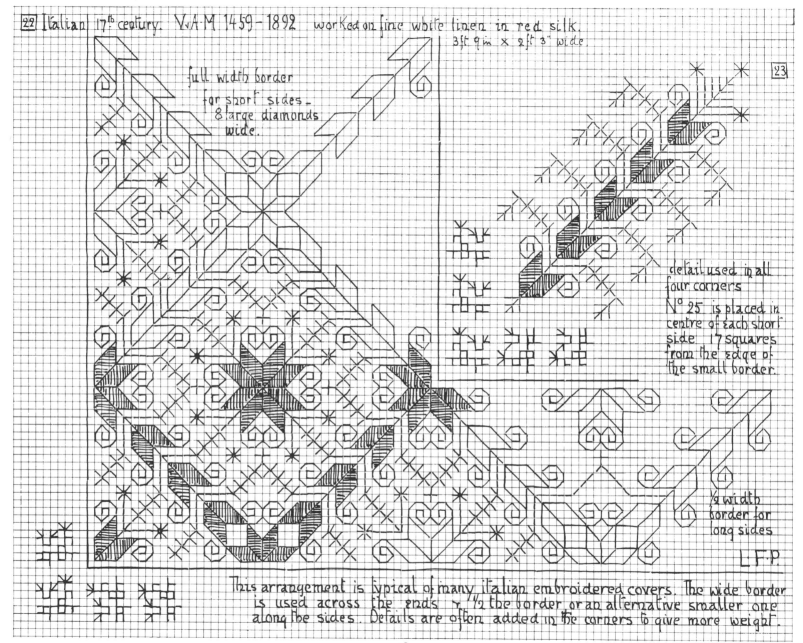

22 Italian 17ᵗʰ century V.A.M 1459-1892 worked on fine white linen in red silk.
3ft 9in x 2ft 3" wide.

full width border
for short sides.
8 large diamonds
wide.

23

detail used in all
four corners

Nº 25 is placed in
centre of each short
side 17 squares
from the edge of
the small border.

½ width
border for
long sides

L.F.P.

This arrangement is typical of many italian embroidered covers. The wide border
is used across the ends & ½ the border or an alternative smaller one
along the sides. Details are often added in the corners to give more weight.

24

25

26

27

28

Detail used
in centre of
short side of
design on
page 14

back
stitch

V. A. M. 1459 - 1892

Nos 26 - 27 - 28
are Italian &
belong to
A. M⸰ Daniels Esq.

Worked on
fine white linen
in red silk
The line stitch
outlining the
geometrical satin stitch
is good & gives a distinct
character to the work.

Green

yellow

mauve   pink

Yellow

mauve

All over design from a small Italian cushion
worked in floss silk; flowers alternately mauve
& green on one diagonal and lemon yellow
and pink on the other
diagonal.

Worked in cream silk on
linen with deep yellow
in petals of large flower
& centre of bud.

← this comes 6 squares
below border — then red & white
lace and fringe cp Portfolio III plate 106

L·F·P

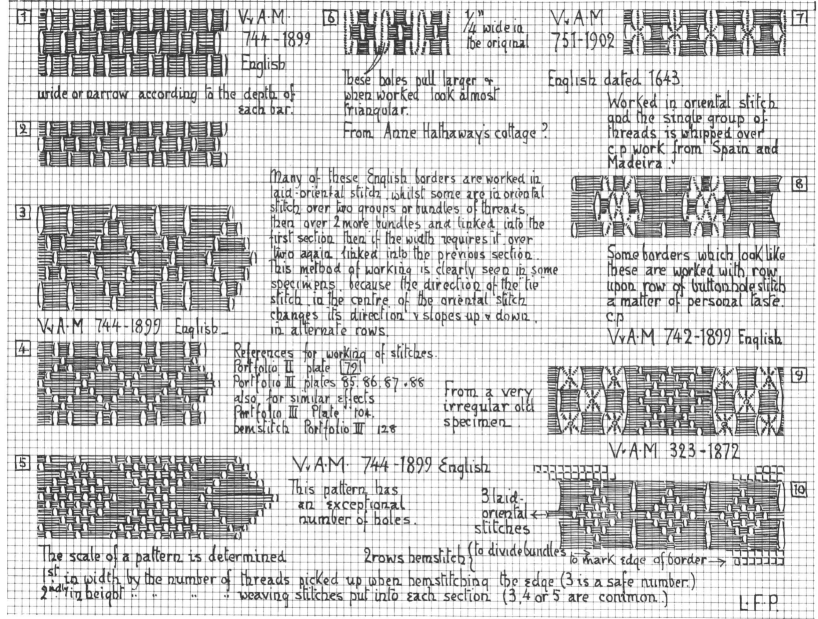

1

V.A.M.
744 - 1899
English

2

wide or narrow according to the depth of each bar.

3

4

V.A.M 744 - 1899 English

5

6

V.A.M

These holes pull larger & when worked look almost triangular.

From Anne Hathaway's cottage ?

Many of these English borders are worked in laid oriental stitch, whilst some are in oriental stitch over two groups or bundles of threads, then over 2 more bundles and linked into the first section then if the width requires it, over two again linked into the previous section. This method of working is clearly seen in some specimens, because the direction of the "tie stitch" in the centre of the oriental stitch changes its direction & slopes up & down in alternate rows.

References for working of stitches.
Portfolio II plate 79
Portfolio III plates 85, 86, 87, 88
also for similar effects
Portfolio III Plate 104.
hemstitch Portfolio III 128

V.A.M. 744 - 1899 English

This pattern has an exceptional number of holes.

¼" wide in the original

V.A.M
751 - 1902

English dated 1643

Worked in oriental stitch and the single group of threads is whipped over c.p work from Spain and Madeira.

7

8

Some borders which look like these are worked with row upon row of buttonhole stitch a matter of personal taste. c.p

V.A.M 742 - 1899 English

From a very irregular old specimen

9

V.A.M 323 - 1872

3 laid oriental stitches

2 rows hemstitch ⟨to divide bundles

10

to mark edge of border →

The scale of a pattern is determined
1st in width by the number of threads picked up when hemstitching the edge (3 is a safe number.)
2ndly in height " " " weaving stitches put into each section (3, 4 or 5 are common.)

L.F.P

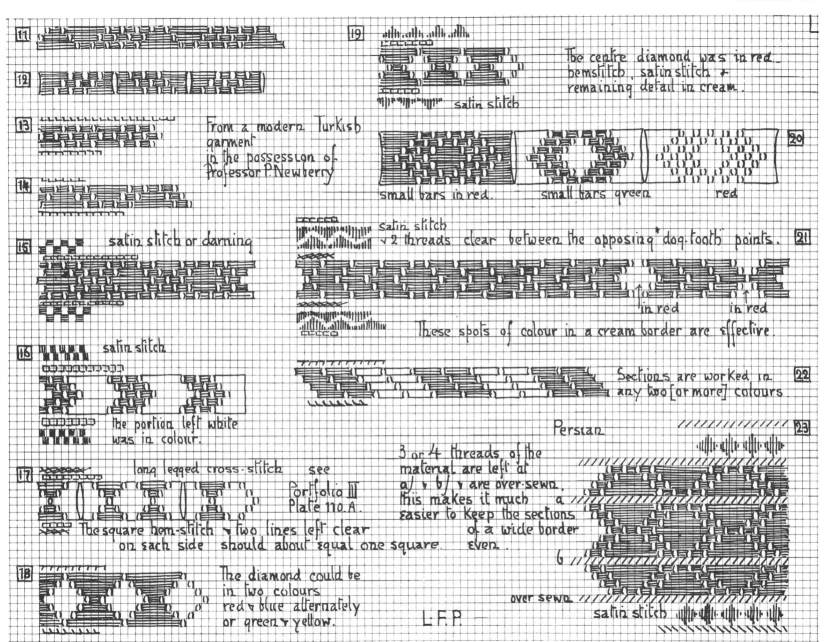

11

12

13 From a modern Turkish garment in the possession of Professor P. Newberry

14

15 satin stitch or darning

16 satin stitch

the portion left white was in colour.

17 long legged cross-stitch see Portfolio III Plate no. A.

The square hem-stitch ⋎ two lines left clear on each side should about equal one square.

18 The diamond could be in two colours red ⋎ blue alternately or green ⋎ yellow.

19 The centre diamond was in red hemstitch, satin stitch ⋎ remaining detail in cream.

satin stitch

20 small bars in red.   small bars green   red

21 satin stitch ⋎ 2 threads clear between the opposing dog.tooth points.

in red   in red

These spots of colour in a cream border are effective.

22 Sections are worked in any two [or more] colours

Persian

3 or 4 threads of the material are left at a/ ⋎ b/ ⋎ are over-sewn. this makes it much easier to keep the sections of a wide border even.

23

a

b

over sewn

satin stitch

L.F.P.

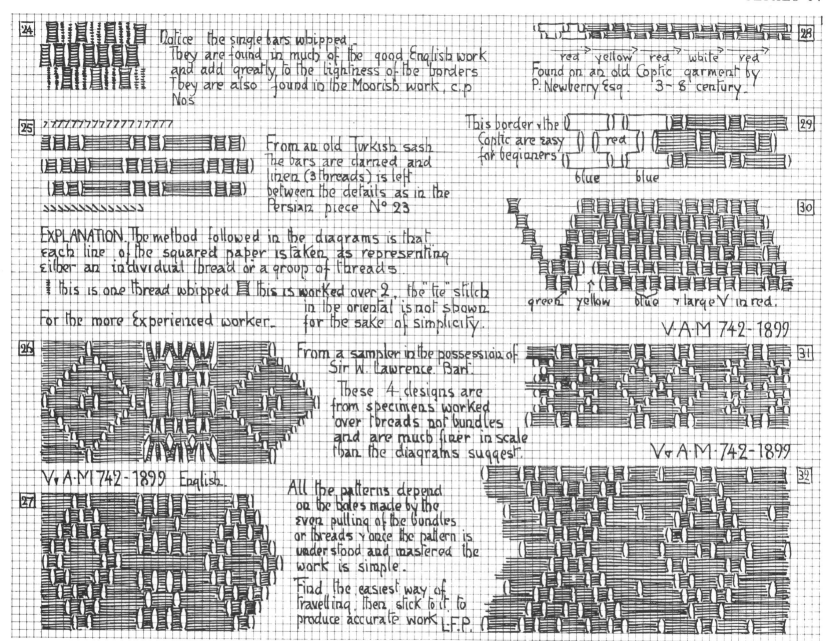

24 Notice the single bars whipped _
They are found in much of the good English work
and add greatly to the lightness of the borders
They are also found in the Moorish work, c.p
Nos

28 red > yellow > red > white > red >
Found on an old Coptic garment by
P. Newberry Esq. 3 - 8 century.

25 From an old Turkish sash
The bars are darned and
linen (3 threads) is left
between the details as in the
Persian piece N° 23

29 This border & the 0
Coptic are easy () () red
for beginners ()   ()
blue   blue

EXPLANATION. The method followed in the diagrams is that
each line of the squared paper is taken as representing
either an individual thread or a group of threads.
⫴ this is one thread whipped ▤ this is worked over 2, the "tie" stitch
in the oriental is not shown
For the more experienced worker _   for the sake of simplicity.

30 green yellow blue & large V in red.
V.A.M 742-1899

26 From a sampler in the possession of
Sir W. Lawrence. Bart.
These 4 designs are
from specimens worked
over threads not bundles
and are much finer in scale
than the diagrams suggest.

31 V. A. M. 742-1899

V. A. M 742-1899 English.

All the patterns depend
on the bars made by the
even pulling of the bundles
or threads & once the pattern is
understood and mastered the
work is simple.
Find the easiest way of
travelling, then stick to it to
produce accurate work L.F.P.

27

32

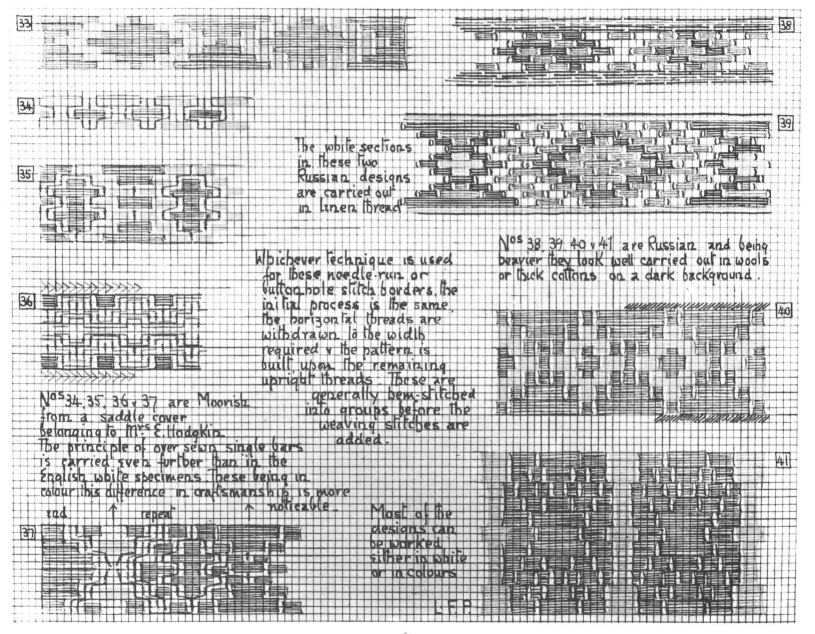

The white sections
in these two
Russian designs
are carried out
in linen thread"

Nos 38. 39. 40 v 41 are Russian and being
heavier they look well carried out in wools
or thick cottons on a dark background.

Whichever technique is used
for these needle-run or
button hole stitch borders, the
initial process is the same,
the horizontal threads are
withdrawn to the width
required v the pattern is
built upon the remaining
upright threads. These are
generally hem-stitched
into groups before the
weaving stitches are
added.

Nos 34, 35, 36, v 37 are Moorish
from a saddle cover
belonging to Mrs E. Hodgkin.
The principle of over sewn single bars
is carried even further than in the
English white specimens These being in
colour this difference in craftsmanship is more
noticable.

end   ↑   repeat   ↑ noticable.

Most of the
designs can
be worked
either in white
or in colours

L.F.P.